God Is With Us

ADVENT

2016

Scriptures for the Church Seasons

ADVENT

2016

God Is With Us

ROBIN WILSON

An Advent Study Based on the Revised Common Lectionary

Abingdon Press / Nashville

GOD IS WITH US
BY ROBIN WILSON

An Advent Study Based on the Revised Common Lectionary

Copyright © 2016 by Abingdon Press

ISBN-13: 9781501820526

16 17 18 19 20 21 22 23 24 25—10 9 8 7 6 5 4 3 2 1

MANUFACTURED IN THE UNITED STATES OF AMERICA

Contents

Introduction

It is time for Christians to live like the coming of Christ into this world actually matters to us. Each Advent season, the church offers us these weeks at the beginning of our Christian year to remember that we worship a God who loves the world enough to become flesh and walk on this earth. Our God walked and talked among us in the person of Jesus Christ to teach us through his life and through his death about the depth of his love for the world. This incarnate God lived as a refugee in a foreign land, associated with sinners and outcasts, befriended both men and women, and reached out to religious elites and those outside his faith. He endured arrest, physical torture, humiliation, and death, all to save the world. The liturgical season of Advent grants us the space at the beginning of our Christian year to remember and to anticipate the One who is the Messiah. The One who has come to save us from our sins. The One who comes to offer hope to the world. We get these weeks to remember that God is with us.

But come on. Who has time for Advent? There are gifts to buy, bills to pay, obligatory visits to make, overtime hours to clock, and end-of-the-year reports to complete. For many, it is a time for parties, recitals, concerts, and any Christmasy event that the culture deems "en vogue" this year. This is the time of year where sentiment about Christmas and nostalgia for the memories of Christmases past can overwhelm the holy wonder and anticipation that is our gift during this liturgical season. For many Christians, no longer is Advent a season about pondering the coming of the One who will save his people. Instead, Advent has become a time to buckle down and endure the stressful additions to our lives until Christmas is finally over.

Where is our faithful witness in that kind of living?

There is a God who loves us enough to send the One into the world who will walk among us and show us, with his life and with his death, how much God loves this world. It is time, this Advent, to slow down and experience the wonder of the coming of the Christ into our world and show the world that Jesus actually matters. Our eyes should light up with anticipation of the joy that comes from knowing that the One who comes to bring salvation to the world is approaching! As we prepare to celebrate the natal entrance of Jesus, the moment when God came in human form and dwelt among us, we cannot help but wait for the return of Christ who promises to come again for his people. And as we wait, God is with us.

This Advent, this hurting world needs the church to live life differently. Advent is to help our finite minds begin to grasp the incredible reality that God is with us. From the beginning of creation through the covenant with Abraham, the admonitions of the prophets, and the granting of kings, God was always with God's people. Throughout our biblical history, God proves God's faithfulness to us, and the Scripture readings offered this Advent remind us of that sacred truth. In the ancient Scriptures from Isaiah, we see a God who provides hope for people that relief will come, that a savior will come, and that God is with them. In the Epistle readings, we see the Holy Spirit moving in that early church, with faithful leaders who remind folks that there is no time to waste! Unite in belief and act like you believe in the Christ! For God is with you! And in the Gospel readings, we see the need for people to prepare their lives to receive the One who will come to usher in a new Kingdom. God is with them.

Just like the people of old, maybe we don't know how to "wait" well. Perhaps that's why Advent seems like the pre-Christmas sprint instead of the holy time it should be. The Scriptures in this portion of our lectionary remind us that there is One who will come to restore, rescue, judge, or save us. God's people at all of these times heard that they needed to wait well as they anticipated a messiah. They needed to live in such a way during this waiting period that their lives were pleasing to God. Loving God and neighbor stand at the top of this list of habits for holy living for the people of God. Additionally, they were to realize that even in their waiting, God was with them. They were never alone or abandoned. God was always at work in their lives and in their world, even in their times of suffering or trial.

This Advent, people need to know that we can wait well for the Messiah, for God is with us. We need to hear that waiting well is not living the pre-Christmas stress the world would impose, but taking the time to worship and love God while serving neighbor, as we ponder what it means to sacrifice ourselves in praise and thanksgiving to a God who comes to save. And we can have the courage to live life differently than the world this Advent, for God is with us. We are never alone. We are loved, called, and strengthened by the God who is always found faithful to God's people.

This gives us the ability and confidence to live differently this Advent. This gives us the joy that the world would steal away in the rush toward another holiday. And this God who is with us deserves to be glorified in our living.

So this Advent: Act like our God really matters. Instead of shop, stress, dread, rush, and worry, choose to worship, reflect, pray, study, serve. Show the world what it means to live like God is with us.

A Reminder of the Future

Scriptures for the
First Sunday of Advent
Isaiah 2:1-5
Romans 13:11-14
Matthew 24:36-44

There is hope, people! Hope that cannot be defeated by war and exile, hope that cannot be overpowered by lulls in faithful living. Hope that cannot be crushed by fear of the future.

This first Sunday of Advent, Christians need to hear hope proclaimed from every pulpit. To get the congregation to feel that holy hope, the preacher only need read the words of Isaiah 2:4 aloud:

> God will judge between the nations,
>> and settle disputes of mighty nations.
> Then they will beat their swords into iron plows
>> and their spears into pruning tools.
> Nation will not take up sword against nation;
>> they will no longer learn how to make war.

What a powerful reminder that God has always had a vision of hope, with creation restored for God's people.

And this God continues to share this hope with the people of the new covenant. Our Epistle and Gospel readings are reminders to the first followers and the early church to be purposeful and deliberate in their faith every day. There is no time for lazy Christianity or half-hearted discipleship. It is time to wake from sleep and to live intentionally loving God and loving neighbor. For God's future offered to us through the Messiah is one of salvation and redemption! It is the ultimate reason for our hope, and we wholeheartedly pursue life within the kingdom of God.

And our God who showed us the Kingdom through Jesus offers us hope in the form of warnings. God sent the prophet Isaiah to his people with a message and a warning. God sent Jesus to warn his people of how to live. And the Spirit of God sent the apostles to keep the early church on task.

God cares enough to send hope and words and direction to God's people throughout time. God still cares enough to give us hope for our tomorrow.

These words call God's people out on our behaviors and hold us accountable for our choices not to condemn us, as if we will shape up and act better out of fear. Instead, each passage this week comes from the ultimate hope that we will experience God's glorious future. For God loves us enough to warn us. We get a glimpse of the glorious future, and we are alerted to prepare ourselves in all ways to be found faithful to be a part of this future. God cares. God really cares. God cares enough to warn us, cares enough to send reminders of our future in case we have forgotten. God reminds us of who we are called to be. There is hope, no matter how wretched we think we are . . . we are loved.

NEW WAYS
ISAIAH 2:1-5

The first chapter of Isaiah contains some hard words. Describing a desolate state for the people of Judah and Jerusalem, the prophet depicts these as God's judgment against the nation for their sinfulness and injustice. Just look at some of Isaiah's condemnations in this chapter:

> This faithful town has become a prostitute!
>> She was full of justice;
>> righteousness lived in her—
>> but now murderers.
> Your silver has become impure;
>> your beer is diluted with water.
> Your princes are rebels,
>> companions of thieves.
> Everyone loves a bribe and pursues gifts.
>> They don't defend the orphan,
>> and the widow's cause never reaches them.

Therefore, says the LORD God of heavenly forces, the mighty one
of Israel:
Doom! I will vent my anger against my foes;
    I will take it out on my enemies,
    and I will turn my hand against you.
I will refine your impurities as with lye,
    and remove all your cinders. (Isaiah 1:21-25)

In other words: You deserve all destruction and humiliation that
befalls you. Ouch. What a harsh beginning.

In Isaiah Chapter 1, the prophet speaks such violent words of God's
condemnation and disgust to Judah that it is hard to read. No one
likes hearing what they've done wrong, having someone list their
wrongdoings, or learning that they deserve exactly what has happened
to them. The people of God were surely cringing and cowering after
God's divine tirade, replete with such harsh language as:

Doom! Sinful nation, people weighed down with crimes,
    evildoing offspring, corrupt children!
They have abandoned the LORD,
    despised the holy one of Israel;
    they turned their backs on God. (Isaiah 1:4)

Isaiah makes it clear that the people of God deserve any destruction,
humiliation, or abandonment that might befall them, setting the
scene and delivering a clear and compelling case for God's justified
destruction of Judah and Jerusalem. It is with a sigh of relief, then,
that we turn to Chapter 2 of Isaiah and hear about a redemptive path
for Jerusalem and the people of God. They will not be destroyed or
wiped out; God is gracious enough to offer them a new path, a new
way forward. After a bit of God's refining, no longer will evil ways be
the way of God's people. Justice and righteousness will be the way of
the people of God. There is hope for a better day. There is hope for
a better way.

That is the hope of Advent: the hope for a better way. It is the hope
that all of our individual and collective evils are not the way life will
continue to be. We can see a vision of how life can be better, and
that the faithful can live into that righteousness. Isaiah 2:1 tells of
what Isaiah sees regarding Judah and Jerusalem, and Isaiah's vision

is glorious. He offers hope to a people undeserving of this graceful opportunity. In the days to come, the "mountain of the LORD's house" will be the highest of all, and "peoples will stream to it."

Mountains are important throughout our Old Testament history, and indeed into the New Testament, as places where people encounter God. Mount Sinai is where God appeared in the burning bush and revealed the divine name to Moses (Exodus 3:1-4, 13-15). It's where God later made a covenant with the whole people of Israel, giving them the Ten Commandments and other laws and instructions (Exodus 19:1-24:8). It's also where God gave instructions for building the Tabernacle and its instruments, so God's presence might go out from Sinai to be among the people of Israel as they traveled (Exodus 25-31).

We also recall the Sermon on the Mount, where Jesus gave new teaching to God's people (Matthew 5–7), or the Transfiguration, where Jesus was revealed in glory before his closest disciples (Matthew 17:1-7). In the New Testament as well as the Old, mountains often become places where people encounter God.

In our passage from Isaiah, it is the temple mount in Jerusalem, Mount Zion, that the prophet envisions. So this new vision of Isaiah, Amoz's son, is that *Gentiles*, foreign nations, would be streaming up to the holiest of places to meet Jacob's God!

Whoa. The new path, the new way, includes Gentiles? Foreigners? The unclean, unwanted people? This is a different vision of life after God's restoration (see 1:26). Up to now in Isaiah, the prophet has been speaking about God's covenant people in Judah. Now the gentile peoples, the other nations, will be drawn to Jacob's God. No longer just the Israelites, but the gentile peoples will also want to learn God's ways and walk in God's paths. Here we see the inherent appeal of this God of power, reaching beyond just the covenant people. It is a shocking concept of a "new way." But at least the people were not destroyed, which seemed imminent in Chapter 1.

But this new way looks promising. It is interesting to notice that the wish of the gentile peoples is to learn God's ways and walk in God's paths. God offers instruction and settles disputes between nations (2:3-4). The result is a peace beyond comprehension. The unfathomable response to the gentile peoples meeting Jacob's God is shocking:

Then they will beat their swords into iron plows
and their spears into pruning tools.
Nation will not take up sword against nation;
they will no longer learn how to make war. (2:4)

God, who made the case through Isaiah in Chapter 1 of how evil and wretched the covenant people were, did not give up on them. Instead, God let them see the world through divine eyes. It is a world of peace and hope, with God reaching new people. It is a world different and new. Then, after seeing what God can do for others outside of the covenant, Isaiah offers the captivating invitation to God's people into this new world of hope: "Come, house of Jacob, let's walk by the LORD's light." After seeing what God can do for those other nations, after observing the peaceful ways of the gentile peoples who are responding to their God, Judah is invited to come and walk in God's light as well.

This good news is a joyous thing to preach to the church this Advent. In my tradition, it would be easy to link this to God's prevenient grace that goes before us. God is always beckoning, calling us to respond even when we are unable or unwilling to do so. The God of Jacob is calling all people to the mountain to encounter God. God still reaches out to every person with love and grace, calling them to learn God's ways and walk in God's paths. God's grace is open to all people today. Indeed, sometimes it is when God reaches the "outsider" that the "insiders" hear God's call afresh and anew in their own hearts.

Isaiah reminds us during this Advent season that God does not give up on God's people. God sends messengers of hope (like Isaiah) with visions of a new way, yet with the same ancient invitation: "Come. Let us walk by the LORD's light."

What new visions might God have for you or your community? How is God calling you to learn God's ways and walk in God's paths?

GET BUSY
ROMANS 13:11-14

Most pastors and priests have that friend: the one who loves to give them funny religious presents. Now mind you, these gifts are never given maliciously, to hurt or to offend; they are simply gifts to remind us church workers not to take ourselves or our churches too seriously. These presents may make us smile, but we probably won't put them on display in our offices! Over the years I have received a bar of soap with instructions how to "wash your sins away," a Jesus action figure, and (most recently) a well-known portrait of Jesus with the added caption, "Jesus is coming. Look busy."

That last gift hit a little too close to home, for we Christians know that feeling all too well. When the teacher walks by our desk, the boss pops in unexpectedly, or the head coach drops by a workout, we all want to look busy. We want to appear as if we have been doing the right thing all along. "Of course, teacher, we have completed all of our homework assignments." "Of course, boss, we have been industrious and diligent with our work." "Of course, coach, we have been working out and staying in shape." And if we have not, we try to fake it, because we know exactly what we should have been doing. And yet, a little warning before they showed up for a visit would have been nice.

In a grace-filled way, this passage in Romans 13:11-14 gives a gentle warning from Paul of what the Roman church already knows. Now is the time to "wake up from your sleep" (13:11) and behave appropriately as people who live in the day (13:13). Paul writes these words at the end of a long description of what new life in Christ looks like (Romans 12:1-13:14). He tells his readers to think of themselves as a part of one body of Christ, echoing his language in 1 Corinthians 12 (Romans 12:4-8). He tells them to love "without pretending" (12:9). He tells them to repay good for evil, welcoming strangers and blessing those who harass them (12:13-17). He reminds them to live at peace with everyone, refusing to seek revenge (12:18-21), and he admonishes them to respect earthly authority (13:1-7). In other words, what Paul writes to the Roman church is an overview of the life that they must now live as a community that has been made new in Christ. Near the beginning of that section, Paul tells his readers, "Don't be conformed to the patterns of this world, but be transformed by the renewing of your minds so that you can figure out what God's will is—what is good and pleasing and mature" (Romans 12:2). Be transformed by the renewing of your minds. Paul envisions a full transformation of the ways we act, live, even think, in the world. In today's passage, Romans 13:11-14, he gives a powerful reason for exhorting them to live in this way. "The night is almost over, and the day is near. So let's get rid of the actions that belong to the darkness and put on the weapons of light" (13:12).

In other words, Paul reminds the Roman church that now is the time to get it together and act. Of course, they know this already. Just like a lazy student who knows the class rules, a careless worker who knows the boss's expectations, or the slacking athlete who knows the need for daily exercise, the Roman church knows what they are supposed to do as children of light. They are baptized believers who have previously "dressed themselves with the Lord" as they have become followers of Christ. They have encountered God and know of his goodness and grace. They are the church, trusting in the righteousness of God. But rarely does knowledge of something assure appropriate action in response. Just because we know we are to love our neighbor, does not mean that we do it. Just being told to pray for our enemies does not send us to our knees. Just because we know that cigarette smoke causes cancer doesn't mean that no one smokes. Likewise, just because the church in Rome knew to avoid the actions of darkness does not mean that they chose the "weapons of light" (13:12).

Perhaps this Advent season our churches can begin to see their reflection in the words of Paul. The Roman Christians may have become comfortable and relaxed, sleepy even, in their faith as the expected return of Christ was not immediate. Many in our churches today have been Christians a long time. They may have lost the fire and zeal that they felt when they first came to know this righteous God who came for the salvation of the world. The urgency and passion to live life showing the love of Christ by serving their neighbor could have easily waned. Perhaps the Roman church has lapsed in showing this love; perhaps our churches today have fallen asleep and forgotten to "live in the day" (13:13).

Verse 14 of this passage reminds the church, "Dress yourself with the Lord Jesus Christ, and don't plan to indulge your selfish desires." The word "plan" is significant as we read this passage today. As we make our plans in life, how many of our plans are about our own wants and desires rather than about preparing ourselves for a life honoring and glorifying God? What are the things we take time to plan in our world today? Do we plan our schedules to worship? Do we calendar around our time we have carved out to pray? Do we order our lives to serve our neighbor? More than likely, we plan around the things that give us momentary and temporary pleasure. We plan for education and work. We plan for family and vacation. We plan for lots of things that make us happy . . . but we have not been intentional about planning for a life that glorifies and praises our God. The call of our desires looms large when we have fallen asleep in a complacent faith.

Thankfully, the season of Advent serves as our wake up call. Advent reminds us of who we are and what is at our core as believers. It calls us to prepare for the coming of the Lord. It is the blessing of Advent to remind us what we already know: We are called to live what we believe. It places things in right order. It boldly declares to us: You know how to live. . . . Act like it. Jesus is coming. Get busy! You've been warned.

What do you spend your time planning for? How much of your energies go into planning how you will serve God each day?

DON'T WORRY, GET READY!
MATTHEW 24:36-44

"It takes a great deal of preparation to appear this carefree." These are the words I tell any new staff who join our ministry team at church. At this point in life I just own my quirks and foibles, including this one: I hate unnecessary surprises. In ministry and life, there are always surprises that come along, and of course one can never fully prepare for anything. But if there is something that I can plan for, if there are actions that I can take in advance, materials I can gather, or arrangements that I can make, that is my preference. That is why this passage of Scripture both raises my anxiety and somewhat soothes me at the same time. For it tells what to expect and how to plan, while also plainly describing what cannot be known. This passage serves as a warning, a tiny glimpse into the future, even if that glimpse tells me, "no one knows."

This passage in Matthew's Gospel serves as a warning to the people of God with a bit of imagery that conjures up scenes from a bad horror movie! Jesus recalls the narrative of Noah (Genesis 6–9), reminding people that if they do not prepare for what is to come, they will be meet a fate analogous to the disastrous Flood! For Matthew's audience, there is grace in being warned about what might happen in the future, since the opportunity to prepare is offered to the hearers. This warning is not from a frustrated and exasperated God, like the warning of a parent who bellows, "If you don't stop right now, I'm grounding you for life!" Instead it is a warning provided to save us! For Jesus lays out what is going to happen. He tells us what to expect with the coming of the Human One. He offers a solution to avoid the outcome: Get prepared.

God loves God's children enough to give them a heads-up! God wants them to be ready and gives them a warning: "Hey, make sure you aren't too preoccupied with the things that you do everyday that you forget to include God!" This teaching of Jesus functions much as a lighthouse beacon keeps ships from crashing into rocks on a shoreline. He warns us to stay off the rocks, to be prepared in our spiritual lives to welcome the Human One when he comes again. He warns us to not be so preoccupied with ourselves, our daily routines, and our busy lives that we make no room for spiritual growth. The people of Noah's time were going about their lives, "eating and drinking, marrying and giving in marriage," with no clue that everything was about to be swept away (Matthew 24:38-39). We must learn a lesson from them, because the Human One will come just as suddenly as the Flood. We must be a people who are constantly ready to welcome God into this world. Wow! How incredible that our all-powerful God cares enough to give us this reminder to be prepared.

There is a bit of a paradox, however, because even as Jesus warns his hearers to be ready, he tells them that they cannot know the day or hour of the Human One's coming. Of course we will be prepared if we know in advance when something can happen. We can cram for the exam, or secure our belongings before the storm, or stay awake and catch the burglar in the act. It's much more difficult to stay prepared all the time. And yet that is how Jesus calls us to live.

There is also, however, a word of reassurance in Jesus' words. "Nobody knows when that day or hour will come." While this statement could be another moment of raised anxiety for the hearer, it could also be of great

GROUP STUDY GUIDE

Questions for Discussion

1. In our Old Testament passage, we find that people from outside of the covenant are drawn to God. Where do you see people today who are often considered "outsiders" to church, who seem to be showing that God's grace is at work in their lives?

2. What shape does God's grace take for these persons?

3. The reflection above mentioned that encounters with God often happen on mountains in the Scriptures. Where do you encounter God more often or in a deeper way than elsewhere? What would it mean if you started seeing church "outsiders" coming to meet God alongside you in these places?

4. Christians and churches today are often accused of not speaking up or acting in response to evil and injustice in our world. What are the things that we know that we should do but fail to do as Christians today?

5. How have we Christians grown comfortable and complacent in our faith today? Where have we lost our passion for loving and serving our neighbors?

6. Where are you asleep or lazy in living your faith? How do you need to wake up in faith and live what you believe in your community or in our world?

7. People often think of getting ready or getting prepared as a chore. How are Christians called to prepare ourselves spiritually to live in this world according to the will of God? How can we as Christians model spiritual preparation as a joy, not a chore?

8. How do we go about our daily lives not preoccupied with an end, but occupied with our task on earth that will fit us for the end?

9. Do we as God's church today still believe in the God who casts new visions? What would change about the world if more people were to learn and long to walk in God's paths?

10. How can you open your eyes more to God's new visions? How can you open someone else's eyes to God's ways?

Suggestions for Group Study

Pray the Psalm Together

Begin your session with a responsive reading of the Psalm for this week. The group leader should read the portion in regular print, with the rest of the group reading the bold text.

Psalm 122

I rejoiced with those who said to me,
    "Let's go to the LORD's house!"

Now our feet are standing
    in your gates, Jerusalem!

Jerusalem is built like a city
    joined together in unity.

That is where the tribes go up—
    the LORD's tribes!

It is the law for Israel
    to give thanks there to the LORD's name,

    because the thrones of justice are there—
    the thrones of the house of David!

Pray that Jerusalem has peace:
    "Let those who love you have rest.

Let there be peace on your walls;
    let there be rest on your fortifications."

For the sake of my family and friends,
    I say, "Peace be with you, Jerusalem."

For the sake of the LORD our God's house
    I will pray for your good.

Spiritual Gifts Inventory

A spiritual gifts inventory is an assessment that people can complete about themselves to help them identify their spiritual gifts, the special talents and desires that they can share in ministry with the church. Some can be taken online, and others can be found online to be printed and used in a small-group setting. You can find more information about spiritual gifts inventories, with links for ones to use in your group, at the following websites:

- *www.umc.org/what-we-believe/spiritual-gifts-online-assessment*
- *www.umcdiscipleship.org/resources/diy-tools-for-spiritual-gifts-discernment-and-ministry-deployment*

Invite group members to take a spiritual gifts inventory, preparing copies in advance for your group to use or ensuring that they can take the inventory online.

Allow each group member to name his or her spiritual gifts that were identified, and encourage the group to celebrate and affirm these gifts.

1. How have you seen evidence of each person's gifts that were identified in the assessment? How have you seen God using these gifts to work through each of us?

2. Were any of the gifts that you discovered for yourself surprising? Why or why not?

3. What might God be calling you to do with this new awareness of how God is with you?

4. How can we use our spiritual gifts within our congregation or community? How can we work together to support one another in nurturing these gifts?

Say a prayer thanking God for your spiritual gifts and asking God to help these gifts to grow within you and find an outlet in the church and in the world.

The Means of Grace

The Methodist tradition of Christianity identifies "means of grace" as ways God works in the lives of Christian believers. Prayer, Scripture reading, corporate worship, meditation, fasting, doing good works, visiting the sick, generous giving, and other practices open us up to God and can serve as avenues through which we experience God's grace.

Brainstorm with your group about the means of grace that they have engaged in or experienced. What are the key avenues through which they typically experience God's grace?

Listen especially for the following examples, and be sure that you mention them if nobody else does:

Prayer
Scripture reading
Worship
Holy Communion
Fasting
Visiting those in prison
Caring for the sick
Tithing
Serving others
Singing hymns and spiritual songs

Discuss with your group how these means of grace—habits and practices of Christian community—help us grow spiritually. Ask the following questions:

1. Out of the ones we have listed, which means of grace is the most powerful for you? Why?

2. In which of these practices do you often struggle to see God's grace?

Instruct your group to form pairs (with one group of three if there's an odd number), and divide the various means of grace among the pairs. Give two, three, or more means of grace to each set of partners until they have all been assigned.

Invite each set of partners to discuss how each of their means of grace helps them to grow spiritually and experience God's love and transformation. Allow 5–10 minutes for these conversations to take place, then invite each set of partners to share their conclusions with the rest of the group. Ask the following question to the group as a whole:

How can these means of grace prepare us to receive Christ this Advent? How can they enable us to live here and now, walking faithfully without knowing the day or hour when Christ will return?

Invite each group member to choose one means of grace that you have discussed and practice it purposefully throughout this week. Ideally, this will be something they have never tried before, or that they have not engaged in recently. Remind them that this can be a way to open themselves to God in a new way.

Closing Prayer

Almighty God, we are tired in life. We are tired of work; we are tired of leisure; we are tired of merely existing day to day without true fulfillment. Inspire us again, dear Lord, to live with joy and purpose. Free us from our preoccupation with ourselves, and light your holy fire under us once again. May we actively pursue you, who came into the world to save us. For it is in Jesus name we pray. Amen.

A Better Way

God's future for us and for the world is greater than we can ever imagine. But sometimes, the circumstances of our present make that future hard to envision. God surely created this world to be better than the world we see reported on the news: a world of war, a world of political manipulation, a world of economic exploitation, a world of senseless violence, a world of greed and ambition.

These passages in week two of our Advent journey allow us to see for a moment into the kingdom of God. We see those glimpses of how life could be when we read of Isaiah's message of a Coming King, who will offer a peace that passes anything we can imagine. We dare to hope for a time when the body of Christ is unified in the church Paul addresses in Rome. And we hear of the coming of Christ who judges and protects his own. In each of these Scriptures, our souls should rejoice in relief and joy, for the powers of this world will not win!

So why is it so difficult for us as Christians to put our whole faith and trust in out God? Even when we see those moments of God's action in our midst, why do we still fail to believe that Christ really came to save the world? In many churches, the Lord's Prayer is prayed each week, and the earnest plea is for "thy kingdom [to] come, thy will [to] be done on earth as it is in heaven." If millions of Christians have been praying this for years, why would we not believe God can bring that peace, that comfort, that joy on earth, as it is in heaven? Do we believe that unity, peace, and hope can possibly be ours?

In the Isaiah passage, God provides that Kingdom—an unbelievable state of peace in the natural and human world, by the Lord's Spirit through the Davidic line. In the New Testament and Gospel passages, followers are invited to live in the Kingdom by their repentance, following the One who was coming and glorifying God by choosing to live in unity. God provides the Kingdom, and then invites us to be a part of it and live it on earth, as it is in heaven. It is our choice whether or not to have enough faith and confidence in our God to live into God's way of showing forth the Kingdom. No wonder so many of our congregations keep praying the same prayer week after week. . . . After all this time, we haven't quite gotten it right. Proclaim it this Advent, with your words and with your life. Believe that Christ offers us a better way.

INNOCENCE RESTORED
ISAIAH 11:1-10

I think we have a vegetarian in our house. Recently, this conversation happened at the dinner table between my husband and my son, over a plate of fried fish.

"Dad, why do they name foods after animals?"
"What do you mean, son?"
"Why do they call fish, 'fish'?"
"Because it is fish. . . . "
"It's what?"
"It's fish."
"Like fish that swims in the water?"
"Yes. It's a fish."
"Oh, gross. That's disgusting."
"But you love fish."
"But I didn't know I was eating a real fish!"
[pause, as he looks to his sister's half eaten plate of chicken] "What about a chicken leg?"
"Yeah, that too. It's a chicken's leg."
"That's horrible!"
"Why do you think it's called a chicken leg?"
"Because it *looks* like a chicken's leg!"
"It *is* a chicken leg!"
"That's disgusting. We eat chickens? How do they get the bone out?"

"They don't. That's the hard part."

"That's a bone?"

"Yes, a bone. What did you think fish and chicken were?"

"Just different kinds of meat."

"But all meat comes from animals."

"It does? What about steak?"

"It's from a cow."

"Ham?"

"A pig. And bacon, too."

"Bacon's a meat? I didn't know that!"

"Are you being serious?"

He has eaten a lot of cheese, raisin bread, and yogurt since then.

It is a cruel moment where innocence is lost, when we realize that we live in a world where wolves eat lambs, snakes bite children, and indeed, many humans eat animals. It is another cruel moment when we learn that there is poverty, injustice, and oppression. In our world, people are starving, homeless, exploited, and abused. There is pollution and war; there is depression and misery. It is a harsh place.

In election years such as this one, candidates often set themselves up as the triumphal leader who will bring back the good old days: when everyone was prosperous, there was no war, communities were free from the threat of violence, and all children were happy. At least that's what the commercials lead us to believe. As idyllic scenes of lush lawns, happy families, beautiful sunsets, and patriotic banners invade our screens, there is an intentional nostalgia invoked for a simpler, more harmonious time.

Which is, of course, never the full truth.

Isaiah prophesied to a people who knew of war and threat and danger. The Assyrian army had run strong and violently all around them. The stories of war and exile of the Northern Kingdom at the hands of the Assyrians in Isaiah's day surely made their way to Judah. And the people of Judah and Jerusalem faced the very real possibility that the Assyrians would conquer and destroy them as well. There was no innocence or naiveté about the world anymore.

To these people, Isaiah speaks this word of great hope. There is a leader coming. There is One who will lead with authentic faith and righteousness (verse 5). The Spirit of the Lord will rest on him, and under his rule everything will change. Had they made political commercials in ancient Judah, the leader who rises from the root of Jesse would have spawned unbelievable ads. And he would live up to the glorious hype.

It is the restoration of innocence. One can picture the Garden of Eden, before the fall, when hearing these words from Isaiah,

> The wolf will live with the lamb,
>   and the leopard will lie down with the young goat;
>   the calf and the young lion will feed together,
>   and a little child will lead them.
> The cow and the bear will graze.
>   Their young will lie down together,
>   and a lion will eat straw like an ox.
> A nursing child will play over the snake's hole;
>   toddlers will reach right over the serpent's den. (11:6-8)

It is a peace that passes all human understanding, an overruling of survival instincts, the overcoming of fear, and the lack of threat. Interactions change at the most basic, fundamental, biological level.

It is a new vision, a new hope, when the One from the Davidic line comes with the Lord's spirit.

During the season of Advent, as people are growing weary of hearing political leaders tear each other down while glorifying themselves, and as Christians are pondering anew what it means to have hope in the One who is to come, we can draw strength from Isaiah's good word that God's future for God's people is beyond our wildest dreams. It is more than we could ever have hoped for.

With the coming of this peaceful kingdom led by the root of Jesse, there comes the amazing hope that other nations "will seek him out, and his dwelling will be glorious" (Isaiah 11:10). Much like last week's Old Testament passage, this passage keeps before us the theme of other nations being drawn to the covenant people and their God: This time, it is through the root of Jesse. The faithful, righteous, Spirit-of-the-Lord-led leader will attract and compel outsiders to follow.

The glorious vision of hope and peace in a new Kingdom is a message that we need to hear. For God never leaves God's people. God always offers a brighter vision for tomorrow than we even dream is possible. God's power overcomes the brokenness of a fallen world and offers a new way forward. The world will be made new. God is with us.

How is your community looking for a messiah today? Do you place your faith in a political candidate, in a spiritual leader, in a community leader, or in someone else? How is your faith shaped by the hope of the new Kingdom?

THE WITNESS OF WELCOME
ROMANS 15:4-13

Welcome each other.

On my first Sunday as the newly-appointed pastor, there were thirty-five people in the worship service. One was my father, who sat on the back pew and was told that he needed to move—he was in somebody's seat. The small congregation in rural Alabama had a long and storied history. A pastor who opposed integration led the majority of the congregation to leave the denomination during the civil rights era. They had seen religion rip their community apart. Those who left the denomination and formed a new church kept possession of the church building, while a faithful remnant worshiped in the basement of the local library. Years later, the state supreme court returned the church building to the rightful congregation, and this once-full, proud congregation now hosted only a few worshipers. But the faithful remnant had a heart for people of all ages, nations, and races, and embraced all . . . well, almost all. As the years progressed, they hired someone to lead them in ministry with the many persons who migrated from Central America to work in the local chicken plant. They had multi-cultural Bible school in the community and in the church building. They served Christmas dinner (together with the local Muslim community on Christmas Day) to anyone in the community who wanted to attend, or they took meals to people in their homes. They taught Sunday school to disabled persons in a group home near the church.

To my chagrin, there were only twenty-nine people in church my second Sunday, including my district superintendent! This led me to investigate where everyone was. It was a small town; they couldn't have that much to do on a Sunday! What I discovered was fascinating: those not in attendance didn't feel welcomed or wanted anymore by those who were still actively involved in the worshiping community. Somehow, there was a disconnect between those heavily involved in these aforementioned ministries and those who were not.

If I had only thought to preach this passage back then! Paul's writing alludes to an unhealthy dichotomy among the early band of Christians: those who were Jews and those who were Gentiles. He does a little recap of who God is and in so doing encourages both factions. He reminds them all that the God of the Hebrew Scriptures is the God who made covenant with the Jews first. Yet through Jesus Christ, God's salvation is open to all. All are loved. All are welcome. All are family. . . . so glorify God by welcoming each other! Everyone, let down your guard and love! Remember how Christ loves you? Love each other and give a little bit!

That's what Paul said to this early church. It's not about you; it's about God. This Scripture passage stands at the heart of what Paul is saying in this letter! All of God's work through Israel showed the nations who God is, so that the Jews were a light to all peoples. Now, to the followers of Christ, with their diverse backgrounds and understandings of faithful living, he writes: Go live in such a way that you welcome each other and glorify God.

Amazing things began to happen. People came back to church. As they came back, they were embraced and welcomed. Attendance and ministries grew, and people from outside the church began to notice the ways God was working in these internal relationships as well as in the way they were reaching out to the larger community. This church that had split so long ago expanded its ministries to those in need. It also took in new members who were the descendants of those who left over the issue of social justice and race so long ago! Anglo, African American, and Hispanic church members worshiped in this historic building and joined together in the vows of baptism. We ordered our lives after the example of Christ that all children would be surrounded by steadfast love, established in the faith, and confirmed and strengthened in the way that leads to life eternal.

They remembered who they were . . . all of them. Together in life and in ministry, they witnessed to their faith to a hurting world.

This was Paul's goal for the early church: that they would glorify God in their unity. For as it is written: "May the God of endurance and encouragement give you the same attitude toward each other, similar to Christ Jesus' attitude. That way you can glorify the God and Father of our Lord Jesus Christ together with one voice" (Romans 15:5-6).

May ours be a witness of welcome, united and faithful, this Advent season.

Who within your church family might feel unwelcome, unwanted, or unneeded? How can you reach out to them?

NOW HEAR THIS
MATTHEW 3:1-12

A friend checked in with his elderly mother by phone. The conversation turned to the mother's church, which had recently welcomed a new pastor. It seems his enthusiastic and evangelical style was not what this traditional, rural church was accustomed to. Apparently, when the sermon came around, the new pastor stepped out from behind the pulpit and walked up and down the aisle with lots of hand waving and loud preaching. He wanted that congregation to repent of their ways and receive Christ again into their hearts and lives, every Sunday. His demonstrative delivery was reinforcing his message with each week's sermon, or so he thought. When my friend asked his mother, "How is the new pastor working out," she replied, "He's got lots of religion, but if they will leave him over here for a while, I think we can get it out of him."

That sounds a lot like good old John the Baptist, who doesn't step back from telling people that they need to change their ways. There is nothing like hearing good ol' religious folks being called "children of snakes" to get us ready for the joy of Christmas. This is John, the locust-eating, wilderness-living oddball who has the nerve to disrupt the usual and familiar religious rhythms of the day. John barges into our beautifully appointed churches with the poinsettias, Chrismon trees, Advent wreaths, and well-planned worship talking about snakes, axes, and burning husks. It's almost like those who compiled the lectionary don't know how awkward this is for people planning worship in the twenty-first century!

Surely, John was so radical, so different, that people paid no attention to him. But we find that instead of running *from* John, people in that day were coming *to* him. In verse 3, Matthew reminds us that the people saw he was the one prophesied in Isaiah who would prepare the way for the Lord (Isaiah 40:3). There was something about this strangely dressed man and his abrupt and direct message that compelled people to come to him, confess their sins, and be baptized. "Change your hearts and lives!" was his call. "Here comes the kingdom of heaven!" (Matthew 3:2). His message, his sincerity, his truth were so compelling that people came to him.

In our world today during the Advent season, we Christians are called to hear the modern day message of John the Baptist. We must recognize that there is One whose sandals we are not worthy to carry. There is One coming who requires lives to be completely turned to him. There is One coming who calls us to proclaim the gospel and make his paths straight. Perhaps we can relate to that new preacher who got so fired up that he could not conform to the expectations of the religious folks in the pews. We must hear John's hard message and then in turn pass it on to a world that will struggle to receive it. By our lives, we point the way to the One who comes to separate the wheat from the husks, storing the wheat in the protection of a barn and burning the husks with a fire that can't be put out! Like those who first heard the words of John the Baptist, must feel the weight of the grace-filled, yet judgment-laced message that confronts us. Like John's audience, we must learn how to live for the kingdom of heaven, for the One is coming. Change your hearts and lives. Confess your sins, repent, and live differently.

It is after the Pharisees and Sadducees came to John for baptism, showing no fruit that they were changing hearts or lives, that John tells of the One who will come to separate the wheat from the husks. Repentance, not reliance on heritage, is what is necessary to prepare for the One who is coming. Ouch. That is a hard thing to say during a season fueled by nostalgia. Congregations want to hear the same Christmas carols, watch the same Christmas movies and television shows that are broadcast each year, and have the same traditions in their churches. Preachers know: If you want to be asked to leave a church, go ahead and mess with their Advent and Christmas rituals and traditions in your first year there!

But John the Baptist gives us permission to think differently this Second Sunday of Advent. We need a little John the Baptist in us to share the good news of the One who comes to save and care for a faithful, repentant people. Challenge yourself to receive and respond to the bold word that John brings. And challenge yourself to speak a similar word to someone else who needs to hear it just as much as you do. Show others with your deeds and tell them with your words: "Now hear this! There is one who is coming who 'will baptize you with the Holy Spirit and with fire!'" You've got a message your fellow believers and the rest of the world need to hear. Like the people of old, they will be drawn to this truth and the message they need to hear. Even if it messes up your expected Advent plans.

How are you called like John the Baptist to "prepare the way of the Lord" today?

Truth in Love

1. Confess sins
2. Repent
3. Live differently

Questions for Discussion

1. The peace that is described in the Isaiah passage this week seems almost too good to be believable. How can we today begin to comprehend a peaceful Kingdom as described in Isaiah, when we live in a world with such pain? What do you see in the world that gives you hope for a peace like this?

2. How does the vision of the peaceful Kingdom give hope to our world situation? With the fears and horrors of war, starvation, terrorism, and refugee movements in our society today, how can this passage speak a word to Christian community?

3. Have you ever been a part of a church that was not unified in its mission and ministry? What are some of the things that cause great disunity in a church? How can individuals or churches find healing from this type of brokenness?

4. What draws a church together despite varied opinions about political, economic, and social matters? How do they find unity in God rather than becoming divided by such issues?

5. Where are the tender places that are calling for unity in our churches today? What differences can we put aside to still come together with a united voice to proclaim the good news of Christ to a hurting world?

6. The people came to see John in the wilderness, even though he was different. Why do you think they went? To whom are we drawn today?

7. Who in your life tells you the honest truths about your need to repent and live differently? Or what circumstances do you encounter that cause you to realize these things? What is the value of such brutal honesty? How does God speak to you through such persons or situations?

8. How can we balance bold new proclamation of the coming of Christ with the pressure of established Christmas traditions in worship?

9. Do you think everyone is called to prepare the way for the Lord? How can we as ordinary people live this way in everyday life? How can you tell someone else about Christ as a way of preparing for the Lord?

Suggestions for Group Study

Pray the Psalm Together

Begin your session with a responsive reading of the Psalm for this week. The group leader should read the portion in regular print, with the rest of the group reading the bold text.

Psalm 72:1-7, 18-19

God, give your judgments to the king.
Give your righteousness to the king's son.

Let him judge your people with righteousness
and your poor ones with justice.

Let the mountains bring peace to the people;
let the hills bring righteousness.

Let the king bring justice to people who are poor;
let him save the children of those who are needy,
but let him crush oppressors!

Let the king live as long as the sun,
as long as the moon,
generation to generation.

Let him fall like rain upon fresh-cut grass,
like showers that water the earth.

Let the righteous flourish throughout their lives,
and let peace prosper until the moon is no more.

Bless the LORD God, the God of Israel—
the only one who does wondrous things!

Bless God's glorious name forever;
let his glory fill all the earth!

Amen and Amen!

Just Peace

The vision of unity that we read about in Romans 15:4-13 requires a firm commitment to justice, reconciliation, and community among Christians. One Christian organization, The United Methodist Church's JustPeace Center for Mediation and Conflict Transformation, is deeply committed to this work. Here is the description from their website: "JustPeace is a United Methodist center that prepares and assists leaders and faith communities to engage conflict constructively in ways that strive for justice, reconciliation and restoration of community" (*justpeaceumc.org/*). Look them up online, or contact them to learn more about how this group works for the unity that we read about in Romans 15:4-13. Research the following questions before your group meets, and share your findings with your fellow group members. Or, invite your group to use the Internet to research them during your time together:

1. What is the purpose of JustPeace?

2. How can conflict within churches and communities be costly? How does JustPeace strive to resolve or mediate conflict in healthy ways?

3. What services or resources does JustPeace offer to churches, individuals, and communities as a part of their work?

4. How does JustPeace exemplify the community life that Paul lifts up in Romans 15?

After discussing these questions, brainstorm practical ways in which you can engage in this type of work for reconciliation in your own church and community

Live Out Your Mission

Talk to your pastor or church leadership about the mission of your church. Your church may have a mission statement on its website or available in some other way. This statement ideally provides an overarching, simple statement of your church's purpose and direction. Even if your church doesn't have an official mission statement, your pastor or church leadership should have a sense of your church's mission.

Discuss with your group the church's mission statement and how your church lives this out in its ministry and mission. Read your church's mission statement aloud to the group, or summarize what you have learned from your pastor or other church leader(s). Discuss the following questions:

1. Does this sound to you like an accurate statement of our church's purpose and direction? Why or why not?

2. How well do we as a church live out this mission in our community? What parts of it do we excel at? What could we do better?

3. How does this mission take shape in your life as an individual?

Next, explore how this mission and ministry "prepares the way of the Lord" during Advent and Christmas. Ask the following questions:

1. What shape does your church's mission take during the season of Advent?

2. How can you help in the mission of your congregation in this faithful work?

Identify one key action that your group can take, or that each individual in your group can take, in order to support this mission. Commit to doing this over the next week, and pray for one another as you do so.

Closing Prayer

Loving God, give us the courage to have hope in you—hope enough to believe that your way is the better way—that you offer peace, comfort, joy, and a fullness of life that we cannot imagine. Open our imaginations to begin to glimpse your Kingdom, and grant us the fortitude to place all of our hope in you, who sent your Son to show us your better way. In Jesus holy name we pray. Amen.

Of Course

No matter how secure we are as Christians of the hope that we have in Christ, no matter how solid our faith that our God will save us, no matter how deep and mature our faith that the Holy Spirit moves and works among us in this world, each one of us needs to hear the assuring words that God will save us. In the Isaiah passage this week, we hear of the people of God being able to return joyfully to Zion. We hear of a God who redeems and provides a glorious future for God's people. In James, the followers of Jesus are compelled to step back and marvel at the work of God in their midst and all around them in the world. And in Matthew, people of faith of all generations to come are given permission to ask Jesus, "Are you the one who is to come?"

All of these Scripture passages speak to our desperate hope to believe in the Messiah, but also address our fallen human tendency that needs to hear again and again that God is indeed still at work in this world. God has sent Jesus to continue that work of restoration and wholeness, which can be seen now and in the world to come. We need to know and to be shown that God is near, that we are not alone.

The evidence of God's redemptive and saving work is all around us. These Scriptures remind us that God has always been near and is always at work in our world. But in times of hardship and stress, fear and anxiety, we too, like the people of old need to hear the good news once again. God is moving here. God is acting here. God is working for wholeness and peace here. Of course, God is here. . . . Look again. What a holy and needed word that this world needs to hear this Advent. May we proclaim it boldly.

THE BACKWARD RECORD
ISAIAH 35:1-10

Country music songs characteristically are about hard-working, fun-loving, non-affluent people who are down on their luck. There's an old joke that goes something like this: What do you get if you play a country music song backwards? You get your truck back, your dog back, your wife back, and your job back.

With all of the joy of restoration found in this passage from Isaiah 35, it could be a country music song played backwards. Isaiah has come a long way from his words of judgment against Edom and other nations in the last chapter:

> The LORD rages against all the nations,
>   and is angry with all their armies.
> God is about to wipe them out
>   and has prepared them for slaughter.
> Their dead will be cast out,
>   the stench of their corpses will rise,
>   and the mountains will melt from their blood. (Isaiah 34:2-3)

Or better yet,

> Edom's streams will be turned into pitch,
>   its dust into sulfur,
>   and its land will become burning pitch. (34:9)

When read together, Chapters 34 and 35 provide a striking and vivid contrast. God's judgment and wrath dominate in Chapter 34, yet in Chapter 35, we see that creation itself will rejoice and celebrate when

> the LORD's ransomed ones will return and enter Zion with singing,
>   with everlasting joy upon their heads. (35:10)

When read together, these chapters indeed could be a country song played first forward, then backward.

The restoration of creation and the healing of all infirmity are coming for God's people in captivity. The return of the exiled to their home in Zion is marked with happiness and joy. And it all hinges on the action of God in verse 4:

> Say to those who are panicking:
> "Be strong! Don't fear!
> Here's your God,
>   coming with vengeance;
>   with divine retribution.
> God will come to save you."

Look at the might and power of God on display in this passage! This is the God to whom nature responds with joy and witnesses the divine glory and splendor. This is the God who will come to save God's people. If the God who is coming to save will heal humanity's afflictions and make every place of fear and desolation bubble up with life-giving water, what hope they should have! This God is coming for them, to make a path for them and for them alone. For those who are redeemed, there is no danger, there is no fear. They return joyfully to Zion. It all ends well, for

> Happiness and joy will overwhelm them;
>   grief and groaning will flee away. (35:10)

All that they've lost in exile will be restored.

In other words, they get their truck back, their dog back, their wife back. . . .

This Advent season, it is the joyful responsibility of the church to proclaim the glory and power of the God who comes to save God's people. No matter how bleak the surrounding landscape of life, God sends a prophetic word of hope. Even when the powers of the world have the upper hand, God is more powerful. No matter how bleak the future seems, we are claimed and loved by the God who acts for us. How awestruck we should be at the power of this God who shows favor to these powerless people.

People need to hear that word of hope today. We hear painful, hope-quenching words all the time that tell us about the bad things. We can see these things for ourselves if we look at the world around us: Racism is alive and well. Sins and offenses against others threaten to undo our personal relationships. Injustice prevails in our culture. Innocent people suffer.

Despite these realities, Isaiah bears a different message: God has not forgotten you. God never abandons God's people. Hold on. This suffering is not the end. God will come to save you. God is on your side.

Even though the world tells us every day that there will always be war, that there will always be fear, that there will always be pain, there is hope! God wants to roar over the message that the world screams at us. Racism is surmountable; sin is forgivable; society can be more just; humanity can be redeemed; and suffering is not the end! All of this is because God is sovereign and God is working in this world and promises to be with us!

Your network of relationships will be filled with those who need to hear about this saving God. They are looking for hope, and they do not hear it in the song the world plays. Play the record backward for them. Tell them about the power of our God to heal, to save, to restore, to transform!

Where have you seen God's restorative power in your life? your church? your family? your world? Who needs to hear this holy message of hope that you can tell?

URGENT PATIENCE
JAMES 5:7-10

We have the world at our fingertips. At least that's what it seems like as we hold these extraordinary cell phones that access the Internet at lightning speed. I fear the days are going or gone when students would spend hours researching a topic, with a pile of books beside them in the library. Now we just ask Siri, and she responds with a quick answer to problems. My kids figured out that Siri could solve their math homework if they just asked her to add, subtract, multiply, or divide. She would even tell them how to correctly spell their spelling words! Needless to say, Siri is banned from homework in our house!

But as we look in our communities, it is harder and harder to find someone who does not have their cell phone close by. We are so used to being able to get instant access to the activities of our friends far and wide through social media, the world through news feeds, games to keep us entertained through apps, that it is almost shocking when the Internet goes down. I was in Starbucks one day, using their free Wi-Fi, and their Wi-Fi went down. Suddenly, all these quiet composed people who had been enjoying their coffee sprang into a complaining, whining group of petulant children! They didn't like the extra amount of time their 4G or LTE network took to access the same information and were unwilling to wait. Most people left.

What does it mean to read James's word of patience in a society that is accustomed to instant gratification? By this third Sunday of Advent, I imagine many people are ready to fast-forward to Christmas. Perhaps you are too. Homes have been seasonally decorated for a while, and the tree is beginning to shed. People have been through Advent and Christmas before; they know what is going to happen. They they may even know the gifts they will receive. . . . So the attitude becomes, "Let's go ahead and have Christmas already!"

James combats that quick-fix, easy gratification notion in his time as well. At the end of Chapter 4, James delivers this bombshell to those who are looking for fast profit: "Pay attention, you who say, 'Today or tomorrow we will go to such-and-such a town. We will stay there a year, buying and selling, and making a profit.' You don't really know about tomorrow. What is your life? You are a mist that appears for only a short while before it vanishes" (James 4:13-14).

But there is something about patiently waiting, living a life that does not selfishly look toward a quick reward, which places us in a right relationship with God and neighbor. We are not God, and this world is not about us and our satisfaction or gratification. When we patiently wait, we have the opportunity to look up from our lives (or our phones) and see what other things are going on all around us. We can take notice as the farmer does (verse 7) of the beautiful way God has ordered the world. We learn to appreciate God's rhythm and God's timing, looking forward to the fruit that will be produced not instantly, but with nurture. We learn to give others the grace to grow and mature in faith as we stop complaining about them.

I love that James tells the reader to hurry up and be patient, almost conveying impatience with those who are not yet patient! James gives us the impression that we must be patient soon, because the coming of the Lord is near and "The judge is standing at the door!" (James 5:9).

There is an urgency about the need for God's people to be patient. How's that for a concept?

We have no time in this life to act in an impatient, selfish manner. God's "nearness" to us compels us to see the world as God see it and to live each and every moment glorifying and honoring our God. There is no time for us to continue in the habits and practices of worldly ambition and self-gain. God's nearness compels us to live differently as Christians than the rest of the world around us. There is no time for us to see the world as a playground that produces resources only for our comfort and advancement. God's nearness forces us to see the world differently. It is a place to see God's hand at work, to labor for the gospel, to serve and to worship the one who was and who is and who is to come.

The concept of "urgent patience" is one which should be shared this Advent season. The time is now to look up from our self-absorbed existence and marvel at the world around us. The time is now to stop complaining. There is no need to ease into it. God has called God's people to right behavior and righteous living. It is time now to put into practice what we believe. Advent gives the church these weeks to wonder at God's coming, to right our relationships and our behavior toward one another. These days give us the moment to put into perspective our selfish dash through life, clawing for satisfaction and pleasure. It is time to slow down, look up, and live right. Now. Right now.

Where in your life are you rushing through, neglecting to look up and see what God is doing all around you?

HOLY QUESTIONS
MATTHEW 11:2-11

"Are you the one who is to come, or should we look for another?" Come again? Could John the Baptist really be asking Jesus this?

It is hard to get past John the Baptist's first question to read the rest of the Scripture passage. Last week, we heard John the Baptist boldly calling people to change their hearts and lives! The kingdom of heaven is near. Big bad John the Baptist called the Pharisees and Sadducees "children of snakes." John was the prophet making the way for the Lord, as Isaiah foretold, showing up like a confident superstar, looking like he could overturn the tables of the moneychangers in the temple himself. In Matthew Chapter 3, John baptizes Jesus, albeit reluctantly, feeling unworthy (3:14). And now? Now John is in prison asking the question, "Are you the one who is to come, or should we look for another?" (Matthew 11:3).

To the reader who is well aware of their history, this question does not seem to make sense. In Luke's Gospel John responded and recognized who Jesus truly was even when in the womb (Luke 1:41). Their lives and ministries were inextricably linked, as Matthew revealed John to be, "the one of whom Isaiah the prophet spoke" (Matthew 3:3). How could John doubt that Jesus is the one foretold, the one who would save his people, the Messiah? We could get lost asking ourselves why John asks this question. Was he losing hope? Was he losing his marbles? Was he trying to prod Jesus into action? Were John's disciples, rather than John himself, really the ones doing the asking? Did Matthew just insert the question into the narrative? The truth is, we do not know about John's mental or emotional state, and we don't have to know. It was never about John. John's role was always to prepare the way for the Messiah, and this question of John's does just that! Even from prison, John is (intentionally or unintentionally) preparing the way for the Messiah to be revealed.

Sometimes, a good question reveals enough. It allows an answer that we all need to hear. In the hands of the author of Matthew, John's question becomes an opportunity to showcase once again how Jesus fulfills the Scriptures, showing him to be the Messiah. Jesus responds to John's question by lifting up evidence of God's kingdom breaking in: "Go, report to John what you hear and see. *Those who were blind are able to see.* Those who were crippled are walking. People with skin diseases are cleansed. Those *who were deaf now hear. Those who were dead are raised up. The poor have good news proclaimed to them.* Happy are those who don't stumble and fall because of me" (Matthew 11:4-6). Jesus doesn't answer John with a simple "Yes." Instead, he points to things that are happening, which have been foretold in Scripture. Isaiah says that "the eyes of the blind will be opened, and the ears of the deaf will be cleared" (Isaiah 35:5-6). "Those who were blind are able to see," Jesus says, and "those who were deaf now hear." Isaiah also says that spirit of the Lord anoints the Messiah "to bring good news to the poor" (Isaiah 61:1). "The poor have good news proclaimed to them, Jesus says."

Just as John the Baptist fulfilled the ancient prophecy to prepare the way of the Lord (Malachi 3:1), in Jesus, the messianic prophecies of Isaiah 35:5-6 and Isaiah 61:1 are heard and seen as being fulfilled. Healing, restoration, and wholeness are all signs of the Messiah as expected!

Jesus responds to John's doubt with a clear affirmation, rooted in Scripture and the experience of those being healed, that Jesus is indeed the Messiah. John is not faulted for his doubts, and they actually become an occasion to demonstrate Jesus' identity. That can be a joyful message for those of us who experience doubt.

It is hard to struggle with faith inside a church community. Unwittingly, even the most welcoming faith community can give an ethos of expectation that if you are really a follower of Christ, you do not have lapses of faith or questions about God's saving power. When we grieve, when we hurt, when we feel overlooked, when our memory or body begins to fail, when we feel overwhelmed, when we feel alone, John the Baptist gives us permission from his prison cell to ask Jesus the tough questions: "Are you the one who is to come, or should we look for another?" Are you who they say you are? Can you deliver us? Have you forsaken us? Or should we look for another one, another way to find hope and help and healing from the deepest, darkest pits of despair? Just a word, just a glimpse is all we need. No matter how long we have believed, we need to hear that reassuring word afresh and anew that Jesus is the Christ!

This Advent season, we do all we can to give right and proper worship of the Messiah. But in our worship, can we make room this season to acknowledge our questions and doubts on our faith journey? Where might people in your community be looking for someone to save them, to give them hope, to deliver them? Are they looking to the Messiah, or are they starting to doubt, or is the suffering going on too long that they wonder if they need to rely on someone or something else? Hear them ask those holy questions. Provide that space for their honest cry to their God, who is the only one who can give the hope and reassurance that they need to hear. And then it is the call of the community of faith to point to the signs of the Messiah all around us! Jesus' admonition to John's disciples becomes his admonition to us today: Go report to *them* what you hear and see. There are signs of God's love and power all around. Tell the good news! Help them to see and hear the Messiah.

Who is losing hope in Christ or is vulnerable to losing hope? How can Christians share that hope in the world? Where do you see signs of God at work in our world?

GROUP STUDY GUIDE

Questions for Discussion

1. The passage in Isaiah focused on God's restoration. Where do you see God restoring the world today? What do you believe that God is working to restore in your life?

2. Saint Augustine is often quoted as saying, "Give me chastity and continence, but not yet." This is often attributed to his wilder younger years, when his desires did not match with what he knew to be faithful behavior. In that same line of thought, some people today might pray, "Give me patience, but not yet." Why is patience is so difficult to achieve?

3. Who do you know who shows extraordinary patience? What is it that makes this person patient?

4. In our churches today, how are we called to model patience? How can we show patience during the season of Advent?

5. How do we balance an eager longing for God's restoration with the need to be patient in the meantime? What actions or ways of living can help us to hold this balance?

6. Why do you think John the Baptist began to doubt Jesus' identity? How did Jesus' words reassure him?

7. What are sources of doubt in your life? What reassurance do you find during Advent or Christmas? How can you continue to have faith despite lingering doubts?

Suggestions for Group Study

Pray Mary's Song Together

Begin your session with a responsive reading of Mary's Song. The group leader should read the portion in regular print, with the rest of the group reading the bold text.

Luke 1:47-55

In the depths of who I am I rejoice in God my savior.

He has looked with favor on the low status of his servant.

Look! From now on, everyone will consider me highly favored
  because the mighty one has done great things for me.

Holy is his name.

He shows mercy to everyone,
  from one generation to the next,
  who honors him as God.

He has shown strength with his arm.
He has scattered those with arrogant thoughts and proud inclinations.

He has pulled the powerful down from their thrones
  and lifted up the lowly.

He has filled the hungry with good things
  and sent the rich away empty-handed.

He has come to the aid of his servant Israel,
  remembering his mercy,

just as he promised to our ancestors,
  to Abraham and to Abraham's descendants forever.

Offer Hope

Sometimes people undergo such pain that they are afraid to have hope again that God is working for good, that Jesus really is the one who cane to save the world from sin and death. Spend some time in your group thinking of people in your lives or in your community who have recently experienced pain or some other circumstance that may cause them to lose hope. Do this as a prayerful activity, inviting the group to name these individuals or groups up in prayer.

One way to do this is to identify such persons as prayer concerns, inviting your group to name them beforehand and then leading your group in prayer on their behalf.

Another way to lift up these persons is to enter a time of prayer first, asking God to place on your hearts those who have felt pain and struggle to have hope. Allow a period of silence, during which your group members may speak these names out loud or hold them silently in their minds.

After your group has spoken or reflected on the names of those who need God's hope, pray for God to be near them and bring them hope. Before you close the prayer, ask God to show you all how you can reach out to these persons with words or a gesture of encouragement to strengthen their hope. Leave several minutes of silence at the end, opening yourselves to God's guidance.

After you have prayed, share with one another what you felt God leading you to do in order to offer hope to these persons. Commit to acting on this throughout the coming week.

Voice Your Doubts

Many people are afraid to admit their doubts about faith in God to others, especially to fellow Christians. They think that doubts seem to be a kind of weakness. But that is not always true. Often, admitting and sharing doubt can be a sign of a strong faith, and it can be an opportunity for faith to be strengthened.

Make space for each person in your small group to voice what doubts they have about God or the Christian faith, inviting them to say out loud their biggest or most pressing doubts about the Christian faith. Record these on a markerboard or large sheet of paper so that you can recall them easily in the following discussion.

After each person has named his or her doubt or doubts, discuss the following questions:

1. Which of these doubts seems the most difficult or profound for you? Why?

2. How do you usually respond to your own doubts or the doubts of others? What is your reaction when someone else expresses doubt, or when you discover it in yourself?

3. If our doubts can't be eliminated, how can we live faithfully while still having them? What would this mean for you specifically?

Recognize that these doubts do not mean your faith is weak; even John the Baptist had doubts as well! As you name these doubts, ask for God to strengthen your faith even if the doubts do not completely go away. Take heart from the fact that God is with us no matter what!

Discipleship or Accountability Group

Many support or accountability groups provide safe places for people to talk about their faith journeys, including their low points, in a confidential or covenantal relationship. If you are not a part of one, ask such a group if you might visit to learn more about how they are able to share the parts of their faith journey that are hardest to share with others. Or talk to your pastor about such a group and how you might become a part of one.

You might also talk to your pastor about covenant discipleship groups, their beginnings and how they continue in churches today. You can find out more about Covenant Discipleship Groups at the following website: *www.umcdiscipleship.org/resources/getting-started-in-covenant-discipleship-groups*.

Research this website before your group meeting and share your findings with the group. Or, you may invite your group members to use the Internet during your meeting to research this site, discussing the ways in which Covenant Discipleship Groups can help us support one another and grow in faith together.

Determine with your group if this is something you might want to start in your church, so that people can share their faith journeys together.

Closing Prayer

Almighty God, you have never abandoned your people. Forgive us, God, for feeling hopeless, for forgetting that you are there to walk with us through valleys and shadows. And thank you for never letting us go, even when we doubt you or lose our way. Though we are like the lost sheep, you always will look for and find us. We hold onto that in the hardest of times, when we cling to the hope of a promised Messiah. Love us through our fears and our doubts as you always have; for we pray in the name of Christ. Amen.

Let Me Tell You!

Scriptures for the
Fourth Sunday of Advent
Isaiah 7:10-16
Romans 1:1-7
Matthew 1:18-25

God is here. Now. With us. As we move into the readings in week four of Advent, we feel an excitement about the movement of our God in Scripture and all around us. In Isaiah, we find a persistent God who is so eager to show the people of Judah that he will save them and that he is faithful, he all but overrules the king and insists on showing them that there is hope, whether they want it or not. In the reading from Romans, Paul helps the people in that church remember exactly who they are: "dearly loved by God and called to be God's people." And in Matthew, we find the witness of Joseph, who puts aside any other dreams and aspirations he might have had for a "normal" life and heeds the word he receives from a messenger of God to be a part of the story of Christ.

We learn a lot from what each one tells us. God can't help but tell King Ahaz that there is a sign of hope. Paul can't help but tell the Roman church about the God who has called him. And Joseph's humble obedience can't help but tell us about his faith in the God who calls him to be a part of God's plan.

This season of Advent, what are we called to tell people about the Messiah, the Christ, the Savior of the world? Are we bursting for an opportunity to point to our persistent God who never gives up on us? Are we looking past ourselves to point to the God who claims us and calls us his own? Are we humbly living quiet lives of faithfulness and service as we respond to God? These are all amazing parts of our biblical story. As we too are brought into the celebration and the proclamation of the coming of the Christ, they remind us that there are many different ways to faithfully and authentically witness to the Messiah. The important thing is that we do witness with our lives, with our words, and with our actions. Be challenged by these ancient witnesses. Tell the story.

A NEW HOPE
ISAIAH 7:10-16

In 1977, George Lucas released the first movie of the *Star Wars* saga. The interesting part was that it was the fourth episode in the storyline. It wasn't hard to follow, however; audiences could grasp enough of the backstory to become fully invested in the characters. People accepted that Leia was a princess, Luke an orphan, Han Solo a smuggler, and Darth Vader a devotee of the dark side. Most of us wanted to know a little more, but we weren't going to dig for it. Audiences soon enjoyed Episodes 5 and 6, which moved the characters forward chronologically and also further alluded to a significant backstory. Several years later (beginning in 1999), that backstory took shape as Episodes 1-3 were released sequentially (albeit, with mixed reviews). A generation learned about how the world of *Star Wars* came to be, after already knowing what would be happening in the next episodes. For those of us who grew up knowing Episodes 4–6 (the last being released in 1983), it was impossible to watch the first three without envisioning what was to come. And that's not to mention Episode 7: *The Force Awakens*, which is a whole other topic for us *Star Wars* fans!

For many of us, reading today's Scripture from the Old Testament seems just like the *Star Wars* movies: out of order. We read these verses from Isaiah or hear it proclaimed from the pulpit, and it is impossible for us not to link it to the coming of Jesus, especially since Matthew 1:22-23 quotes this specific passage as the angel of the Lord appears to Joseph. Since we are reading this on the fourth Sunday of Advent, after all, we have the birth of Christ on our minds! The future story has already been written; the prophecy of the virgin birth and Immanuel is fulfilled in the birth of Jesus.

While we know that God sent Jesus to be *the* Messiah, Savior of the World, it is important for us to hear and truly understand this part of the backstory, learning of another time long, long ago when God acted in the world for God's people. And just like *Star Wars* episodes 1–3 versus *Star Wars* episodes 4–6, the Isaiah story may not prove as popular as the story of the Christ Child, but it will give us a richer understanding of the full saga.

When the prophet Isaiah first spoke about the young woman who would give birth to a son (Isaiah 7:14), the rulers of Aram and Israel (called Ephraim) were plotting to attack Judah. The Judean King Ahaz was understandably concerned. The Lord sent word through Isaiah that the attack wouldn't happen (Isaiah 7:1-7), but apparently, King Ahaz remained apprehensive. So God spoke to King Ahaz again, this time telling him to ask for a sign (Isaiah 7:10-11). Ask for anything, God says. Let me reassure you. Let me show you my power. Let me show you that I am with you and that I am trustworthy. This almighty, all-powerful God does not give up, and God will not back away from Judah or let its people down. But King Ahaz will have none of it. When King Ahaz declines to ask for a sign, Isaiah expresses both his and the Lord's exasperation with King Ahaz and Judah's lack of confidence in the Lord.

But exasperation at King Ahaz's tiresome ways does not mean that God gives up. God insists on telling this nervous king that his enemies will not attack and that he can trust that God's words are true. Even though King Ahaz won't ask, even though King Ahaz is irritating, God promises a sign of faithfulness anyway:

> The young woman is pregnant and is about to give birth to a son, and she will name him Immanuel. He will eat butter and honey, and learn to reject evil and choose good. Before the boy learns to reject evil and choose good, the land of the two kings you dread will be abandoned.
>
> (Isaiah 7:14-16)

God doesn't give up on showing the people that God can be trusted. This sign offered is a baby, whose name Emmanuel means, "God with us." By the time this baby is old enough to choose good over evil, these two threatening kings will be defeated and their land abandoned.

We Christians see an additional meaning to Isaiah's prophecy, which Matthew describes for us by showing its fulfillment in Mary's pregnancy and Jesus' birth (Matthew 1:22-23). Jesus, Matthew says, is the one called Emmanuel, God With Us. (By the way, the Hebrew of Isaiah spells Immanuel with an "I," while the Greek of Matthew spells it with an "E." So that's why we see the two different spellings.) But despite the fulfillment of this prophecy in Jesus, the words carried a different meaning for the people of Isaiah's day. We can wonder whether Isaiah or his audience anticipated some deeper truth underneath Isaiah's words, but it's unlikely that they expected a baby to be born to an unmarried girl more than seven hundred years in the future! For them, Isaiah's words provided comfort in the here and now, giving to King Ahaz and others assurance that God was with them, come what may. They had nothing to fear from Aram or Israel. They could trust in God's presence and protection.

In that ancient time of stress and threat, the Lord was there, never failing to offer reassurance and deliverance. The church needs to hear these words today. We know that God is our rock and our salvation. We know that our hope and trust are in the One who never fails. This Advent, when we cannot help but recall with great joy the baby born in Bethlehem so long ago, we can also remember that God was offering hope and deliverance for God's people long before. The prophecy about Immanuel was at the beginning a sign that God was with the people of Judah despite a threat that made their hearts shake (see Isaiah 7:2). When our way of life is threatened and we seek solutions based upon our own cunning and strategies; or when our primary hope is not in the one who came that we might have life, and life abundant; or when do not see the signs all around us that God will ultimately deliver us, let us look back at this passage from Isaiah and remember the backstory of a God who has always cared for God's people. It gives us the confidence to look to our future unafraid (with even more anticipation than *Star Wars* fans had before Episode 7 was released)! There is more to come in this journey of life, and our God goes before us. God is with us. The saga continues, with a new hope.

As you look back over your life, where has God shown you signs that God can indeed be trusted?

A REAL IMPRESSION
ROMANS 1:1-7

Everyone wants to be authentically known—just look at how many people post on social media. We write about what is important to us; we share everyday life; we post pictures and videos; we give our opinions. People long to share themselves in order to be "liked" and to connect with others, even though some might be accused of oversharing at times!

Without the benefit of Twitter, Instagram, Reddit, Facebook, or the social media vehicle du jour, the apostle Paul wrote a letter. Paul had not met this band of Christians in Rome who would receive his letter. They most likely knew him by reputation, whatever that may have been. But in writing this letter to them, he began with these seven verses of introduction that clearly lay out who he was and what he believed.

In the 1980's, Head and Shoulders dandruff shampoo ran an advertising campaign that culminated with the tag line: "Because you never get a second chance to make a first impression." Paul seems to have understood that as well. While following a standard form for a greeting in this letter, Paul takes the opportunity boldly to put his most authentic self forward. He makes a powerful first impression. He introduces himself as a slave of Christ Jesus, an apostle, set apart for God's good news (Romans 1:1). He did not remind them of his occupation as a tent maker, his Roman citizenship, his other name of Saul, his past life as a Pharisee, or his previous persecution of Christians. That was in the past. He now has a new identity in Christ.

Social media gives us the opportunity to introduce ourselves today, and we certainly do not want to make a bad first impression online any more than we would want to do so in person. My daughter was recently allowed to get an account on one of the popular social networking sites, and I cautioned her immediately: "Don't post anything that they can use against you when you run for President!" Now, I don't think the preservation of a reputation or the need to impress his audience would have been among Paul's motives. Paul was forthcoming in other letters about his background (a Pharisee among Pharisees), and he certainly wanted to lead with the present, not the past. But in this letter to the church in Rome, Paul identifies himself theologically, not temporally. His identity is wrapped up in his commissioned task to share the good news. Therefore, he explains his apostolic identity as the result of the good news of God's Son. He speaks of the One promised through Scripture, descended from David, identified as God's Son, and resurrected from the dead (verses 2-4). It is not about Paul; it is about the good news he is called to share, which Paul is much happier to recount in these words of introduction than his human accomplishments, titles, and failings.

This Advent, we can embrace the identity that is truly ours, not just the identity and labels that we have chosen or been given. Paul helps the Roman church name that in verse 7. They are those "who are dearly loved by God and called to be God's people." They are loved and called. So are we. Baptism is the time we receive this new identity, as we put on the person of Christ. We are named and claimed by the One who calls us children of God.

We are no longer identified by past sins, old relationships, or current world-location. For some reason, we are so quick to accept the labels that are given to us by others. We are the good student, the poor kid, the underachiever, the overachiever. We are the nerd, the clown, the sickly kid, the delinquent. We are the cheater, the liar, the unworthy, the gold digger, the opportunist. We are the blowhard, the slimeball, the grouch, the whiner. We are the rich princess, the airhead, the jock, the slob, the thug. We are the Yankee, the immigrant, the foreigner, the hick. We have embraced so many other identities that we forget that we are God's beloved and chosen children! We have forgotten that we are dearly loved by God and called to be God's people. That's all we really need to introduce ourselves to the world. We don't need to try to puff up thinking about how we look on a social media profile or how best to describe ourselves in 140 characters or less. Maybe we can take a lesson from Paul and say instead, "Here's all you need to know about me: Now let me tell you about this amazing, wonderful God!"

During the season of Advent, many people are preoccupied with making a good impression while decorating, entertaining, and celebrating. Somehow, we have allowed this season of preparing for the coming of Christ to be about how we can make everything make a good impression, just like the old shampoo commercial. How freeing it is to read Romans and hear who we are once again: loved by God and called to be God's people.

That is all. And that is enough.

When someone asks you to tell him or her about yourself, what do you talk about? Is your Christian identity mentioned? Why or why not?

A USEFUL LIFE
MATTHEW 1:18-25

The Reverend Jim Dannelly served as the senior pastor of Aldersgate United Methodist Church, and now he remains active in the congregation during his years of retirement. Jim welcomed my husband and me to Aldersgate upon our appointment to serve there together, and he assisted in our knowledge and understanding of that community. I'll never forget the first time I heard Jim preach a funeral. He said a phrase that I heard him use often in the years that followed in giving thanks for the life of a departed servant of God. After opening remarks he would say, "She lived a long and useful life."

Useful? That word seemed almost startling for me to hear. At first, the adjective seemed almost unflattering, like something you might say when you had really nothing good to say about the person who died. After all, we preachers want to lift up the best qualities and characteristics of the deceased, those attributes in which others witnessed the work of God. Surely, more fitting words would be "kind, generous, loving, or joyful." But useful?

Yet, the longer I am in ministry and the further I go in this journey of life, the more I grow to appreciate that word. For that is what we all long to be, isn't it? Useful. We long to live lives that make a difference. We want to help others in their struggles. We ache to play a part in making our family, our church, our city, and our world better. We yearn to be useful with our gifts and our talents, with our wisdom and our enthusiasm.

Matthew makes Joseph useful in the story of the birth of Jesus. Mark and John ignore the birth narrative altogether in their accounts. Luke has Mary as the genealogical link to the Davidic line, as well as her being the recipient of the angel's visit. But Matthew brings Joseph into this important biblical scene. Joseph's righteousness (even prior to being visited by a messenger from God in a dream), coupled with his acceptance of the message that this Child is the fulfillment of the Scriptures, make his role vital to the story of the Christ. In Matthew's account, Joseph links Jesus to salvation history. Joseph has the choice of whether or not to participate in the holy story. Joseph is within his rights to walk away from Mary. Instead, Joseph chooses to live a righteous life within the will of God.

The whole series of events could not have been easy for Joseph: the taboo association with a pregnancy outside of wedlock; the concern about what the future would bring; the responsibility of rearing the Child. And not just any child. The Child will be named Jesus and will save the people from their sins. He is the one of whom Isaiah spoke: Emmanuel, God with us.

It is no wonder that every year when our family gets our Christmas decorations out of their boxes in the attic, Joseph comes out of the attic with a face that looks old and worried. As we carefully unwrap the pieces of our Nativity set and place them into position in the stable, there sits Joseph, holding a walking stick, looking like he carries the weight of the world, not the light of the world.

But Joseph chose to respond to God's message of hope for the world and to take his place in God's story. This Advent, are we ready to take our place in God's story? Are we ready to be the people God needs us to be, so that all will know the Savior of the world is coming? Are we ready to give up our futures, our lives, and our desires, in order to live lives within the will of God?

Many churches pray the prayer below entitled, "A Covenant Prayer in the Wesleyan Tradition," during a covenant renewal service at the beginning of a new year. It is in *The United Methodist Hymnal,* and it remains one of the most powerful prayers congregations voice in unison in worship together. Perhaps we can pray this together at the end of this Advent season, as we ask that God might make us useful and righteous, so that we might take our place in God's continuing story.

> I am no longer my own, but thine.
> Put me to what thou wilt,
> rank me with whom thou wilt.

Put me to doing, put me to suffering.
Let me be employed for thee or laid aside for thee,
exalted for thee or brought low for thee.
Let me be full, let me be empty.
Let me have all things, let me have nothing.
I freely and heartily yield all things
to thy pleasure and disposal.
And now, O glorious and blessed God,
Father, Son, and Holy Spirit,
Thou art mine and I am thine. So be it.
And the covenant which I have made on earth,
Let it be ratified in heaven. Amen. (United Methodist Hymnal, 607)

How are you living a life that someone would call "useful" for God? What gifts do you have to share that could be used for the Kingdom?

GROUP STUDY GUIDE

Questions for Discussion

1. The excitement is building as we get closer to Christmas. Check in with one another and see how you are continuing to prepare your heart and your life to welcome the Christ. Have you become too preoccupied with other obligations, or are you maintaining spiritual practices that help you during this holy season?

2. What do we learn about the character of God in the Scripture passage from Isaiah? What is God like? How do the Old Testament stories like this one strengthen our Christian faith today?

3. As you read the Isaiah passage, how did learning more about the political climate of the day when it was written help you to read the passage differently? How does knowing about the birth of Christ influence how you read the Isaiah passage?

4. Why do we get so worked up this time of year about making everything perfect? Where do you spend your time trying to give a good impression during the Advent and Christmas seasons?

5. Where do you see examples of persons or groups claiming their identity in Christ before any other identity that the world would place on them?

6. How do you see your self-identity? Why is it hard for many to identify as a child of God or follower of Christ above all other titles?

7. Many people suffer from low self-esteem, often because of past failures or perhaps present circumstance. What can we do as the body of Christ to remind people of who they are as redeemed and beloved children of God?

8. What did you know about Joseph before studying our Matthew text this week? How are you inspired by Joseph's story?

9. Joseph's entire life trajectory changed as he chose to be a part of God's story. How is God calling you to change your life and be a part of his work today?

10. Discuss what it might mean to live a useful life. How are we called to be useful as individuals? How are you called to be useful together as a small group? How are you called to be useful as a congregation?

Suggestions for Group Study

Pray the Psalm Together

Begin your session with a responsive reading of the Psalm for this week. The group leader should read the portion in regular print, with the rest of the group reading the bold text.

Psalm 80:1-7, 17-19

Shepherd of Israel, listen!

You, the one who leads Joseph as if he were a sheep.
You, who are enthroned upon the winged heavenly creatures.

Show yourself before Ephraim, Benjamin, and Manasseh!

Wake up your power!
Come to save us!

Restore us, God!

Make your face shine so that we can be saved!

Lord God of heavenly forces,
how long will you fume against your people's prayer?
You've fed them bread made of tears;

you've given them tears to drink three times over!

You've put us at odds with our neighbors;

our enemies make fun of us.

Restore us, God of heavenly forces!

Make your face shine so that we can be saved!

Let your hand be with the one on your right side—
with the one whom you secured as your own—
then we will not turn away from you!

Revive us so that we can call on your name.

Restore us, LORD God of heavenly forces!

Make your face shine so that we can be saved!

Get to Know Joseph

Most study Bibles have a concordance in the back, where you can look up every occurrence of common biblical words, places, and names. Ensure that you all have at least one study Bible with a concordance in your small-group meeting. Or, if someone in your group has a smartphone or other means of using the Internet, you can use a concordance or look-up feature on a Bible study website. Two excellent ones are

- *www.biblegateway.com*
- *www.blueletterbible.org*

As a group, look in your concordance (or online) for every place where Joseph is mentioned in the Bible. (Be sure to distinguish between Jacob's son Joseph in the Old Testament and Mary's husband Joseph in the New Testament. We are talking about Mary's husband.) Put together everything you can find and see what your group can learn about this quiet figure in our biblical history.

Name some of the key characteristics of Joseph that emerge, writing them down on a large sheet of paper, markerboard, or chalkboard. Then discuss the following questions:

1. What stands out the most about Joseph? What surprised you?

2. Compare the role Joseph plays in Matthew's Gospel versus in Luke's Gospel. What differences do you see? What do both authors have in common in the way they portray Joseph?

3. What can you learn from his story? How does Joseph inspire or challenge you as you prepare for Christ this Advent?

4. Do you know anyone personally who exhibits some or all of these characteristics you've identified in Joseph? Where do these qualities seem to come from? How does God work through them?

Covenant Prayer

Invite each of your group members to read the "Covenant Prayer in the Wesleyan Tradition" on pages 68-69 silently. Discuss what it would mean for each of you to pray that prayer and take it seriously. How would that change your lives? Then if your group wishes, pray it aloud together in unison. Discuss the following questions:

1. What was it like to pray Wesley's covenant prayer?

2. As you prayed this prayer, what words or phrases most spoke to you as you communed with God?

3. Were any parts of the prayer difficult for you to pray, or would they be difficult to live out? Which ones? Why?

4. If Christians today were to pray this prayer regularly, what would change as a result?

5. If you were to pray this prayer regularly, what would change in your life as a result?

Encourage your group to pray this prayer to God throughout the coming week, reading it slowly and taking time to let the words sink in.

Closing Prayer

Dear God who knows and loves us fully, let us be fully known to you this day. Know that our actions speak volumes of what our words won't admit: that we are just too busy to prepare much more for you. We know that you will be coming anyway, and we try to take advantage of your grace. Forgive us, and shout a hard word into our souls. If we don't listen, then make us hear you; for we are so excited about your party this December we forgot to find out how you would have us to celebrate you. May we realize who we are and whose we are this Advent, as we anticipate your glorious return; in Jesus' name. Amen.

The Best News

Scriptures for
Christmas
Isaiah 9:2-7
Titus 2:11-14
Luke 2:1-20

Really, you should not be able to mess this up. The news is just too good: A child is born! The Messiah has come! God has come to dwell among us! We are called to celebrate and share this wondrous news. Stick with the basic script, and none of us should botch this.

But what if we have become too predictable in our Christmas Eve and Christmas Day celebration and proclamation? How many years will candles, carols, and Communion cut it? If we churchgoers hear the same story year after year, well, it would certainly be understandable.

These passages give us an excellent chance to take a different look at our old familiar Christmas Eve tune and script. What if we read Isaiah not to see what the coming king would be like, but to see what God has already been doing all along for the people of God? What if we looked at Titus for inspiration and saw that if we believe that Jesus was born and is returning, then we have to live like it? What if we looked at the familiar story of Luke 2:1-20 and noticed the way each biblical character responded? If we looked afresh at the story, might we give our surrounding culture and fellow Christians permission to do the same?

Reverent, beautiful worship is a noble goal for Christmas, but it cannot be enough. The incarnate God revealed in Luke demands a response, and that response can take many forms. The God revealed in Titus, the God who will return, demands a transformed life. The God revealed in Isaiah, who has always acted and will always act for God's people, demands our confidence.

Hear the Word with faith and joy, and then proclaim it boldly with your words and with your life. God is with us. The Messiah has come. It is the best news ever.

GODS AND KINGS
ISAIAH 9:2-7

If you look at pictures of United States presidents from the day they took the oath of office, contrasted with the picture the day they left office, it is easy to see how the task of governing ages a leader. There is one political party always trying to make them seem inept or unfit for office. The pundits and bloggers love to show the highlight reel of every bad decision or contradicting sentence uttered. And anyone with Internet access can now give their anonymous opinion of exactly what they are thinking, twenty-four hours a day. The only one who may have had it worse might be King Ahaz so long ago. With King Ahaz, I imagine he grayed and wrinkled even more than our modern-day presidents during his sixteen years as king. Scripture tells us of his fear of war with Syria and the Northern Kingdom of Israel and his unholy alliance with Assyria (2 Kings 16). God had almost pleaded with Ahaz to trust him, giving him the sign of a child to be born. But Ahaz was not to be deterred from calling upon Assyria, rather than the Lord, for help.

Scholars debate the exact timing of this passage, but a few things are clear. Judah had previously been in a time of "darkness," perhaps a time of death due to hardship, oppression, or war caused by an unfaithful king. And now, the people express joy and give God the credit for rebuilding their nation. The tools and garments of war will be destroyed. That's enough reason to celebrate! But even more, there is a sign that a good and righteous King, like their ultimate hero, David, will come into power! A Child is born who will bring endless peace, who will establish and sustain it (both) now and forever! What hope! Just like the hymn we sing, "strength for today and bright hope for tomorrow," no more unfaithful, God-ignoring, temple-desecrating king for Judah.[1] One is coming who will lead them forward to continue this time of peace: a King of vast authority and great power, a King who will have the title immediately thrust upon him, "Wonderful Counselor, Mighty God, Eternal Father, Prince of Peace."

So how is any new king supposed to live up to all that?

I almost feel sorry for the child or king who comes to live into this label. Many scholars believe the Scripture was referring to Hezekiah, whom the Scriptures remember favorably, but Hezekiah was by no means perfect. No one can be. David and Josiah, the other kings regarded positively in the Books of First and Second Kings, each had their flaws as well. Everyone would have rejoiced greatly if a new king lived up to David's legacy. But in the end, neither David nor his kingdom were without blemish. So despite the high hopes outlined in this prophecy from Isaiah, they had to be a heavy burden for a new king—any new king—to bear.

But maybe this passage is not supposed to be about the new king and what the king can do. Maybe the important words in these verses are the ones we might have overlooked at our first reading, yet those words are the very things that should give us true hope:

- *You* have made the nation great; *you* have increased its joy. (3)
- As on the day of Midian, *you've* shattered the yoke that burdened them, the staff on their shoulders, and the rod of their oppressor. (4)
- *The zeal of the LORD of heavenly forces will do this.* (7)

Look at the bold-print words; look at what God has done! What this beautiful poem tells us is that **God** has acted to save God's people, that **God** is acting in their lives, and that **God** will act long into the future to provide for them. It is the same theme the Lord tried to drill into King Ahaz's head: trust me; let me give you a sign; I am the only partnership you need. In your moments of anxiety and fear, as well as when you rejoice in freedom and deliverance from your oppressors, I will always be your God. King Ahaz never seemed to quite grasp the power of the God who was there for his people. But as we read these words, we might begin to grasp that this season.

Hope is not in a new human king, but in the God who stands with that human king. It is, after all, God who brought success to

Hezekiah, to Josiah, and, yes, to David. It is God who established David's kingdom and secured its future. It is God who protected Jerusalem from its enemies. And ultimately, it is God who fulfilled this prophecy not through a mere human king, but through the birth of God's own Son into our world.

This Advent, especially as so many of those around us are looking to place their hope in a political leader who can never live up to the perfection of any titles we give her or him, let the church remember the One who never leaves us or forsakes us. May we remember the God who has always been at work for us, in good times and in bad. God has always been with us, blessing us, providing for us. No matter our earthly hardships or joys, God is still with us. And there lies our true hope.

When you look back over your experience, how do you see that God has acted in your life? your church? your family?

TAKING JESUS SERIOUSLY
TITUS 2:11-14

This Scripture lesson is a beautiful passage to read on Christmas Eve. . . . But honestly, who uses this in a Christmas Eve worship setting? The Isaiah passage is so familiar and loved, thanks to its inclusion in Handel's *Messiah*. And the Luke passage, well, even Linus reads a portion of it from the King James every year on the annual broadcast of "A Charlie Brown Christmas." On Christmas Eve, Christians will gather to hear about a Baby coming into the world to save us. Churches will light candles, take the sacrament of Holy Communion, and sing carols. Even contemporary worship settings will list towards the familiar on this day of all days, or night of all nights. People unconsciously want to blend their thanksgiving for Christ's natal entrance in Bethlehem so long ago, their reverence for God's active role in their lives and world today, and their eschatological theology that Christ will come again . . . all with a giant heap of nostalgia and tradition.

I propose reading Titus 2:11-14 as the perfect fulfillment of all of those desires, minus the nostalgia and tradition.

The author (a subject of debate, but a debate for another day) writes, "The grace of God has appeared, bringing salvation to all people" (Titus 2:11). This points to the life of Jesus the Christ, who came to this world to bring salvation for all—not just for the Jews, but for all. The implication is that the "all" connotes the followers of Christ, as would be consistent with the rest of the letter (geared as it is toward order of and instruction to the church). Through this gift of grace, the church is to live "sensible, ethical, and godly lives" (verse 12) "as a special people . . . who are eager to do good actions" (verse 14). This is the reason for all of the instruction throughout the rest of the letter to elders, believers, older men, older women, slaves, and Titus himself. Precisely because Jesus gave himself for their rescue and redemption, followers of Christ are to live ethical lives in response to that gift.

And verse 13 recalls the hope the believers should have for the return of Christ. It was not a one-time gift of Christ that they receive; Christ will come again! Their order and sensible, ethical behavior is not all just in response to a gift of long ago; it is how they live in "blessed hope" that the Savior Christ will come again. The people of God were "educated" (isn't that an interesting word here?) by the grace of God through the life and ministry, death and resurrection of Jesus. They are to live what they have learned in order to await his glorious appearance to come.

Live what they have learned.

I wonder what it would mean if all Christians who are packed into churched on Christmas Eve lived what they have learned. This Christmas Eve worship, so many of us already know the basic Christmas story. We knew it when Linus said it again on TV this year. We hear what we want to hear about Jesus coming into the world some two thousand years ago. And then we are ready to go home and get the last minute things ready for tomorrow.

Perhaps we need to hear afresh through the Book of Titus that Christ came into the world, Christ is coming back, and we are to do something in the meantime! I had a seminary professor who challenged his students: "What would it mean to live every day as if Jesus really mattered? How would that affect our churches, our budgets, our calendars, our educational systems? What would we do if the church took Jesus seriously?" So take the message a good bit deeper this year on Christmas. If you know the basic story, remember that it is your joyful responsibility to live like it. It is time to take the Incarnation seriously: The Word became flesh and dwelled among us. God came to Earth! This is REAL! It is world-changing, life-altering stuff we get to live into and tell others about. It is not about manger scenes, candles, and carols. It is about God being here on earth, God's imminent return, and the kind of holy living that we get to do in the meantime.

This Christmas, take Jesus seriously. Blame Titus, blame the season, or blame Jesus himself. After all, this season is all about him anyway.

What does it mean to live like Jesus coming into the world really matters to you? What changes should you make in your life in response to God's gift?

NO WORDS
LUKE 2:1-20

I've never been the first to tell someone about Jesus' birth. Part of that may be my social location; I am from a part of the United States where most residents self-identify as Christian. Part of that may be the excellent job of TV specials, store shelves bursting with Christmas merchandise, and music that begins to take over air waves and elevators around mid-October. And part of it may be the evangelical nature of the "good news." The church has been faithful to share the gospel message; for if you know good news, you can't just keep it to yourself.

If someone who had no knowledge of Jesus read the birth narrative of Jesus in Luke 2:1-7, I wonder what they would think. If they did not know of ancient messianic prophecies or have knowledge of what is to come, would they see the birth as the miraculous incarnational event that it was? I doubt they would be impressed, because this is an utterly unremarkable account of a birth. A couple joins with everyone else to go register for taxes. This couple travels far, to the husband's ancestral town of Bethlehem. If they were at all up on their Old Testament history, they might know that Joseph's being of the house of David could mean something. We keep reading and see that now it's time for Mary to have a baby. She delivers, wraps the baby as parents do, and, since there is no room in the guest room, uses the manger for a crib. That's it.

Notice there is no mention of a messiah; no one calls him Emmanuel, "God with us." No angels are reported. Just a plain account of a poor couple's birth story. We don't even get descriptions of Mary and Joseph's response to this moment in life, nor do we hear any intimate details of what they said or how they felt.

Yawn.

Now, Luke has built up this wonderful scene for us, beginning in Chapter 1, full of highs and lows, emotions and outbursts. There we see Zechariah, "startled and overcome with fear" (Luke 1:12) when an angel of the Lord came to him. We hear of Mary's confusion as she ponders the angel's greeting (1:29). We read that Elizabeth's unborn child "jumped for joy" at the sound of Mary's voice (1:44). We marvel at Mary's praise as she expresses glory to God to Elizabeth (1:46-55). Zechariah praises God (1:64), neighbors are filled with awe (1:65), and Zechariah praises God some more (1:68-79). There is no shortage of expression or emotion that is shared or conveyed, until Chapter 2:1-7.

Excitement picks back up with the shepherds and the Lord's angel. The shepherds were terrified at the angel and the Lord's glory. The angel tells the reader as well as the shepherd who this newborn is! This baby is your Savior! And "a great assembly of the heavenly forces" joined in praising God (2:13-14). The shepherds traveled to Bethlehem and saw Mary, Joseph, and Jesus. They reported what they had heard from the angel of Lord. Only then do we see some emotional responsiveness from those in Bethlehem. Luke tells us they were amazed! Finally, the shepherds leave, "glorifying and praising God" (2:20).

Both the anticipation of and the response to the birth of Jesus are related to the reader with great detail. But the moment when people encounter the God who has come into the world in human form, that intimate moment is too much for mere words. Experiencing the amazing presence of the Holy One, who is given for the salvation of the world, it is beyond human description. We cannot know how Mary, Joseph, or even the shepherds felt when they met the Christ Child.

The "good news" of Christ coming into the world doesn't need embellishment or fanfare. Jesus, Son of the Most High, the one to sit on the throne of his father David, is born of a virgin in the city of David. That's all we need to know, for it is everything.

And now we know that when we meet the Savior, we could react with praise like the angels, with fear and uncertainty like the shepherds, with joy like John the Baptist in the womb . . . or we might find ourselves with no words, just being. Quiet still, in the presence of the promised Messiah. We can come to the Lord in this moment, on this holy day, with any fear, joy, or other emotion we may have, for each of us is given the intimacy with God to come see for ourselves that Christ the Savior has come into the world. And for that, there are no words.

What are some intimate times where you have felt close to Christ in your life? How have you responded? How do you respond now?

GROUP STUDY GUIDE

Questions for Discussion

1. What is your Christmas Eve or Christmas Day tradition for worship? What parts are most meaningful to you?

2. What are the things that you look forward to each Christmas Eve? How do you meet God in each of them?

3. Why do we like Christmas traditions to stay the same? What would it do to us to worship or celebrate differently? What would we stand to lose and gain by doing this?

4. Recall a time when you did not do "Christmas as usual"—when your normal Christmas practices had to change for some reason. What caused the change? How did you experience God differently as a result of something new?

5. As you look at political ads today, how are many of them subtly painting the picture of their candidate as a savior, as a messiah? Are the expectations that we place on candidates fair or unfair? Why or why not?

6. How can we pray for our leaders and for those who might be our leaders, even when we don't agree with their decisions at times?

7. If we place our ultimate hope in Jesus as the savior, how should that affect the way we regard our political and cultural leaders?

8. Why do you think there are so few details about the emotions of Mary and Joseph? How do you imagine they felt during this time?

9. What does the story of Jesus' birth focus on instead of the parents' emotions? What does this say about the significance of Jesus' birth?

10. Find out who is providing Christmas Eve services in your local jail, prison, hospital, or nursing care facility. How can your group help these persons hear this "good news" in these settings?

11. Name all the different persons who saw the Christ Child and went away from the Child in Luke's birth story of Jesus. What was their demeanor? What were their actions?

12. How should we leave on Christmas after celebrating the birth of the Christ Child? What are we called to do differently in response to the birth of our Savior? How can the responses of those in Luke's birth story guide us in faithful living?

Suggestions for Group Study

Pray the Psalm Together

Begin your session with a responsive reading of the Psalm for this week. The group leader should read the portion in regular print, with the rest of the group reading the bold text.

Psalm 96

Sing to the LORD a new song!

Sing to the LORD, all the earth!

Sing to the LORD! Bless his name!

Share the news of his saving work every single day!

Declare God's glory among the nations;
declare his wondrous works among all people

because the LORD is great and so worthy of praise.

He is awesome beyond all other gods

**because all the gods of the nations are just idols,
but it is the LORD who created heaven!**

Greatness and grandeur are in front of him;

strength and beauty are in his sanctuary.

Give to the LORD, all families of the nations—

give to the LORD glory and power!

Give to the LORD the glory due his name!

**Bring gifts!
Enter his courtyards!**

Bow down to the LORD in his holy splendor!

Tremble before him, all the earth!

Tell the nations, "The LORD rules!

**Yes, he set the world firmly in place;
it won't be shaken.
He will judge all people fairly."**

Let heaven celebrate! Let the earth rejoice!

Let the sea and everything in it roar!

Let the countryside and everything in it celebrate!

**Then all the trees of the forest too
will shout out joyfully
before the LORD because he is coming!**

He is coming to establish justice on the earth!

**He will establish justice in the world rightly.
He will establish justice among all people fairly.**

Tell Someone About Jesus

The Christmas story is good news! As we have seen throughout this Advent study, God is with us. That is for us a source of joy, hope, and peace, and it inspires love of God and love of neighbor. It is indeed good news.

This good news—the good news of Emmanuel, God With Us—begs to be told. And yet, so very often we keep it to ourselves. Why? And how can we become the proclaimers of this good news rather than those who hide it? Use the following conversation guide to explore this. Ask:

1. What are the biggest obstacles that stand in our way of sharing the good news of Jesus Christ with someone else?

2. What do we risk when we tell someone else about Jesus, about our faith in him? What risks does it bring about for the other person?

3. What do we stand to gain if we share the good news of Christ? What does the other person stand to gain?

4. What would it mean for you to make proclaiming the good news a part of your life?

Invite each group member to identify persons in your community that you can invite to worship with you, who need to hear the "good news" and celebrate in a Christian community. These can be individuals within your community, or people that group members know personally. Brainstorm ways in which your group could invite them to worship, include them in a meal or shared experience, or otherwise invite them to become a part of Christ's church this Christmas season.

Challenge each person in your group to tell—actually tell, using words—someone about Jesus and the hope they have in him during the next twelve days. You get to be the bearers of this good news to a world that needs to hear it!

Say Thanks

Your pastor, musicians, and other volunteers give a lot of themselves to make Christmas worship meaningful, whether it happens on Christmas Eve or Christmas Day. Often, their families are celebrating without them or waiting to leave on trips until they finish with their worship responsibilities. Think of a way that your group can say "thank you" for their faithfulness to lead God's people to worship the Christ.

You might consider doing something special for them during the next few weeks after Christmas, such as hosting a meal for them. Each person in your group can commit to taking two or three of the staff and volunteers out for lunch, for instance. Or you could invite them all to someone's home and host a post-Christmas party to say thank you.

Another suggestion is to write personal cards or notes to each person who has given time and energy, thanking them for the specific things they have done to lead you all in worship and praise of God this Advent and Christmas. The more specific and personal the note, the better!

If your group is especially outgoing, you might plan to go Christmas caroling, visiting these volunteers and staff to share your favorite songs and perhaps a warm beverage and some baked goodies. Most people expect caroling before Christmas, not afterward, so this will be a bit of a surprise for those you choose to visit!

Regardless of how you choose to do it, know that your pastor, church staff, and volunteers will appreciate your gratitude and recognition of their service this Christmas. This will be a way for you to share God's love of them and help them receive Christ's birth as the good news that it truly is. And it may even start a welcome post-Christmas tradition at your church.

Closing Prayer

How humbled we are to meet you here in this holy moment, gathered with your followers. We are here awaiting your entrance, trying to live lives that are good and useful to witness to your glory, merciful God. As we behold the Christ once again in our lives, in our families, and in our world, may we use all that we are to proclaim to the world the good news of the Christ. May we know the fullness of joy and wonder as we live each day as a gift to you. For it is in Jesus' holy and precious name we pray. Amen.

1. From "Great Is Thy Faithfulness," words by Thomas O. Chisholm. Copyright Hope Music Publishing Company.